Harvey Fierstein (Edna Turnblad)

Left to Right: Laura Bell Bundy (Amber Von Tussle),
Clarke Thorell (Corny Collins), Marissa Jaret Winokur (Tracy Turnblad)

hairspray

Music by Marc Shaiman

Lyrics by Scott Wittman Marc Shaiman

Photos by Paul Kolnik

ISBN 0-634-05349-3

Hal•Leonard® CORPORATION

7777 W. BLUEMOUND RD. P.O. BOX 13819 MILWAUKEE, WI 53213

In Australia Contact:
Hal Leonard Australia Pty. Ltd.
22 Taunton Drive P.O. Box 5130
Cheltenham East, 3192 Victoria, Australia
Email: ausadmin@halleonard.com

Visit Hal Leonard Online at
www.halleonard.com

Left to Right: Kerry Butler (Penny Pingleton), Jackie Hoffman (Prudy Pingleton), Marissa Jaret Winokur (Tracy Turnblad), Harvey Fierstein (Edna Turnblad), Linda Hart (Velma Von Tussle), Laura Bell Bundy (Amber Von Tussle)

Left to Right: Kamilah Martin (Ensemble), Mary Bond Davis (Motormouth Maybelle),
Dick Latessa (Wilbur Turnblad)

Matthew Morrison (Link Larkin)

Marissa Jaret Winokur (Tracy Turnblad), Matthew Morrison (Link Larkin)

Left to Right:
Dick Latessa (Wilbur Turnblad),
Kerry Butler (Penny Pingleton), Harvey Fierstein (Edna Turnblad)

Kerry Butler (Penny Pingleton),
Corey Reynolds (Seaweed J. Stubbs)

GOOD MORNING BALTIMORE

Music by MARC SHAIMAN
Lyrics by MARC SHAIMAN and SCOTT WITTMAN

Oh, oh, oh. Woke up to-day
Oh, oh, oh, Look at my hair. What

feel-ing the way I al - ways do,
"do" can com-pare with mine to - day?
Oh, oh, oh,
Oh, oh, oh,

Hun - gry for some-thing that I can't eat. Then I hear the beat. That
I've got my hair-spray and ra - di - o. I'm read - y to go. The

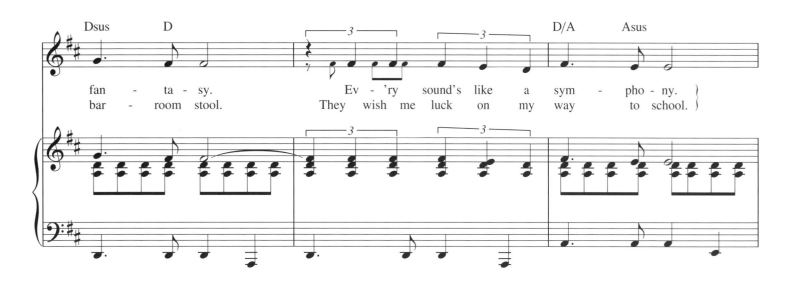

fan - ta - sy. Ev - 'ry sound's like a sym - pho - ny.
bar - room stool. They wish me luck on my way to school.

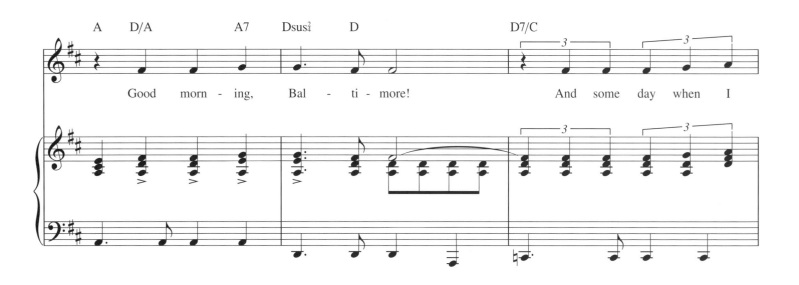

Good morn - ing, Bal - ti - more! And some day when I

take to the floor, the world's gon-na wake up and __ see

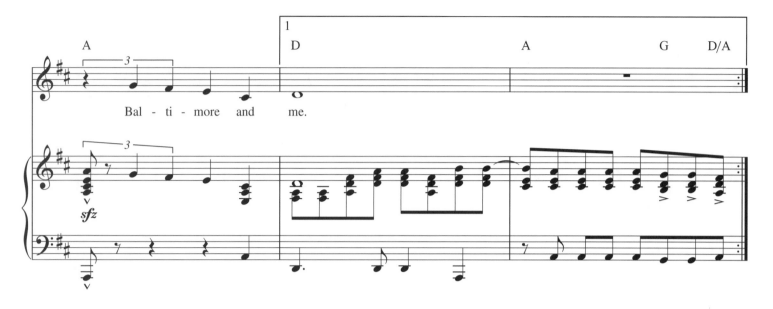

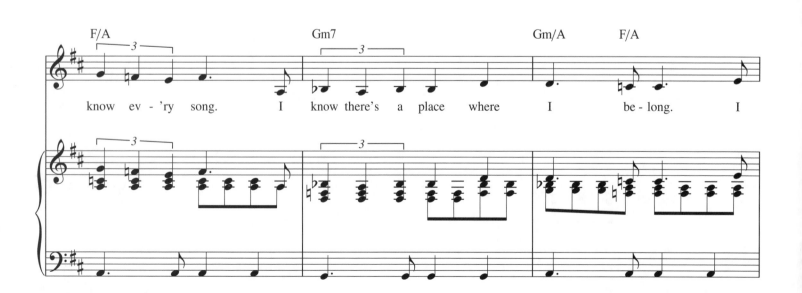

THE NICEST KIDS IN TOWN

Music by MARC SHAIMAN
Lyrics by MARC SHAIMAN and SCOTT WITTMAN

Play bass 8vb throughout

24

MAMA, I'M A BIG GIRL NOW

Music by MARC SHAIMAN
Lyrics by MARC SHAIMAN and SCOTT WITTMAN

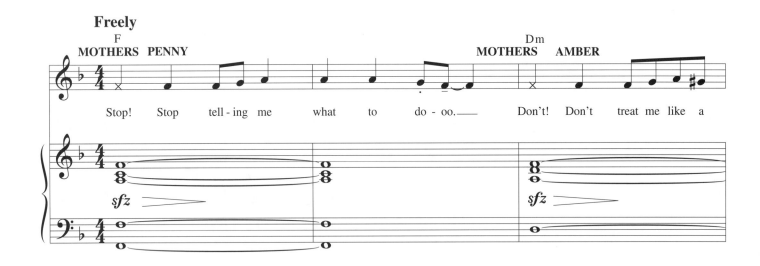

I CAN HEAR THE BELLS

Music by MARC SHAIMAN
Lyrics by MARC SHAIMAN and SCOTT WITTMAN

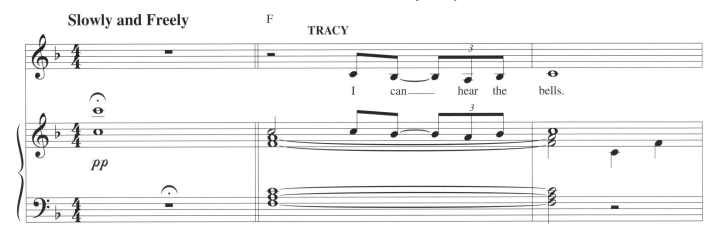

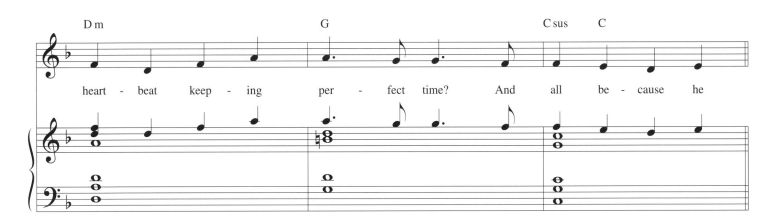

IT TAKES TWO

Music by MARC SHAIMAN
Lyrics by MARC SHAIMAN and SCOTT WITTMAN

They say it's a man's world. Well, that can-not be de-nied.
A king ain't a king with-out the pow'r be-hind the throne.
Just like Frank-ie Av-a-lon has his fav-'rite Mouse-ke-teer,

But what good's a man's world with-out a wom-an by his side?
A prince is a pau-per, babe, with-out a chick to call his own.
I dream of a lov-er, babe, to say the things I long to hear.

WELCOME TO THE 60's

Music by MARC SHAIMAN
Lyrics by MARC SHAIMAN and SCOTT WITTMAN

RUN AND TELL THAT

Music by MARC SHAIMAN
Lyrics by MARC SHAIMAN and SCOTT WITTMAN

LI'L INEZ, SEAWEED & ENSEMBLE

SEAWEED

BIG, BLONDE AND BEAUTIFUL

Music by MARC SHAIMAN
Lyrics by MARC SHAIMAN and SCOTT WITTMAN

Once up-on a time, girl, I was just like you.___ Nev-

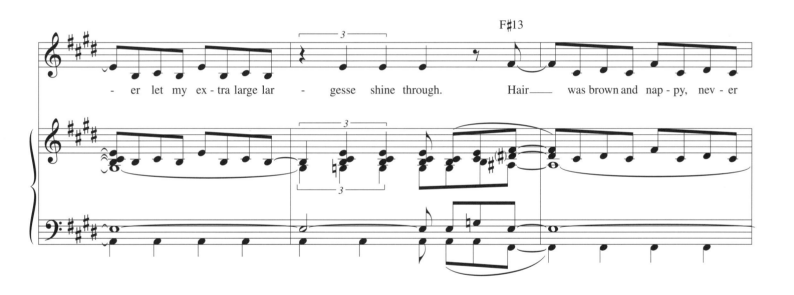

-er let my ex-tra large lar - gesse shine through. Hair___ was brown and nap-py, nev-er

had no fun.___ I hid un-der a bush-el, which is ea-sier said than done. Then___

TIMELESS TO ME

Music by MARC SHAIMAN
Lyrics by MARC SHAIMAN and SCOTT WITTMAN

WILBUR:
Styles keep a-chang-in'. The world's re-ar-rang-in', but Ed-na, you're time-less to me. ____

WITHOUT LOVE

Music by MARC SHAIMAN
Lyrics by MARC SHAIMAN and SCOTT WITTMAN

Bright Rock tempo

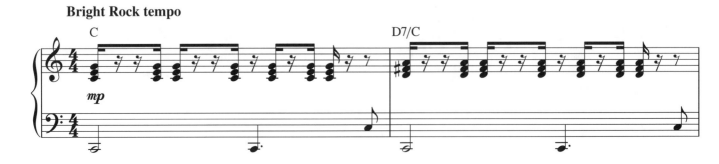

Once I was _ a self- ish fool _ who nev- er un- der- stood. _ I

nev- er looked _ in- side _ my- self, _ though on the out- side, I looked good! _

I KNOW WHERE I'VE BEEN

Music by MARC SHAIMAN
Lyrics by MARC SHAIMAN and SCOTT WITTMAN

YOU CAN'T STOP THE BEAT

Music by MARC SHAIMAN
Lyrics by MARC SHAIMAN and SCOTT WITTMAN

Brisk and exultant

TRACY: You ___ can't stop an av — a - lanche ___ as it ra -
PENNY: You ___ can't stop a riv - er ___ as it rush -

- ces down the hill. ___ You can try ___ to stop ___ the sea -
- es out to sea. ___ You can try ___ to stop ___ the hands _

110

EDNA: You can't stop my hap - pi - ness, __ 'cause I like __

__ the way I am. __ And you just __ can't stop __ my knife __

__ and fork when I see a Christ - mas ham. __ So if you __

try to hold me down, I'm gon - na spit in your eye ___ and say _____ that

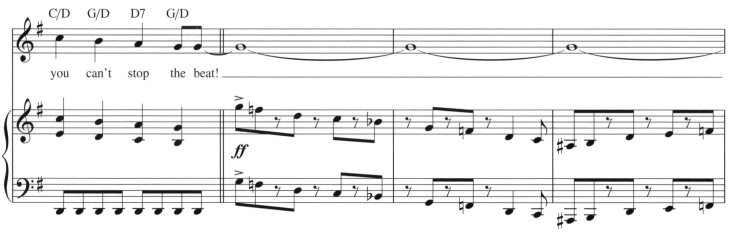

you can't stop the beat! _____

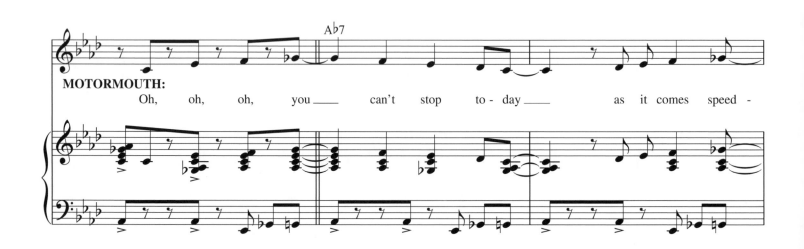

MOTORMOUTH:
Oh, oh, oh, you ___ can't stop to - day ___ as it comes speed -